AF365484

THE POWER OF THOUGHT

The method of healing the inner child and

transforming negative thoughts - The key to success

BY

SILKE RITZEL

TABLE OF CONTENTS

The Objective Of This Book.. 1

Introduction...4

Chapter 1: My Life Path With The Power Of My Thoughts ..8

Chapter 2: What Are Beliefs?..13

Chapter 3: How Do Beliefs Arise? 16

Chapter 4: How Do Beliefs Influence Our Lives?.................20

Chapter 5: Limiting Beliefs And How To Overcome Them 25

Chapter 6: Positive Beliefs To Boost Your Self-Esteem 32

Chapter 7: How Do I Change My Beliefs?............................37

Chapter 8: My Beliefs And Values.......................................44

Chapter 9: The Rich Vs Poor Belief 53

Chapter 10: Parents' Beliefs...70

Chapter 11: Inner Child Work: Heal By Reparenting Yourself
....71

Chapter 12: What Is Spirituality? 84

Conclusion 87

Beliefs Determine Your Life 87

THE OBJECTIVE OF THIS BOOK

I am Silke Ritzel, 55 years old married woman and the mother of two grown children. With my book, I hope to rouse you to consider the following questions.

Who am I? What am I? What am I doing here? The answers to these questions are deeply embedded within you, and everyone has unique answers.

I worked on it for a long time and gradually realized that I needed to change my lifestyle and beliefs to get answers to my questions. Like the vast majority, I had always been on a hamster wheel and had no idea that a completely different path was meant for me and each of us. So, too, set out to discover the meaning of life.

Before I could wake up, I had to go through a major, tragic event in my life. It was only then that I realized I needed to say goodbye to my television first. That was a good thing because from then on, I scoured the Internet and realized that we were being duped in many ways and that life had far more to offer than we could ever imagine.

I began to change more and more. I became independent of everything that worked, whether it was medicines, nicotine, coffee, or whatever, and I also changed my diet from vegetarian to vegan. I became a different person as a result of this diet change. My senses are now much more intense than before. I am completely healthy and content.

I decided to move to the Philippines about three years ago. Unfortunately, my husband was not convinced, so we parted ways with a heavy heart. It was a difficult and brave decision to leave everything behind, whether it was family, friends, or all of my belongings, but no one could stop me now. The decision had been made.

I now followed my heart's desire, which felt natural to me.

When I first arrived in the Philippines, the friendliest country in the world, I felt like I had always belonged here. I've built a new life here and have become increasingly concerned with my "I am." I now had enough time to do so.

My book is meant to inspire you to change your old, negative beliefs into new ones. You will quickly notice that your life will be for the best. I guarantee this inner work will be worthwhile, and you will not be sorry.

Buy this book if you're ready to break free from old shackles and live a happy, self-determined life.

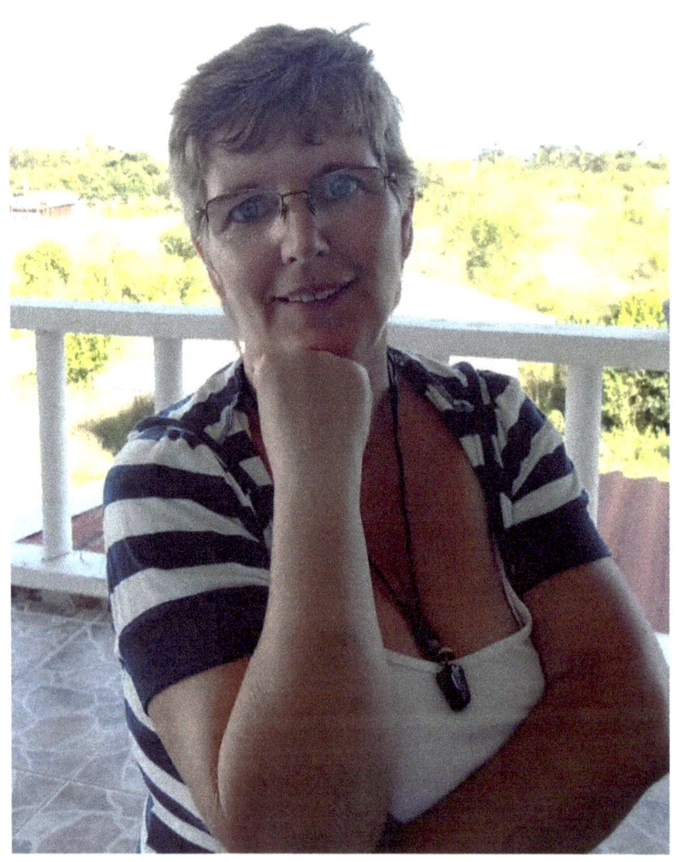

INTRODUCTION

T hinking is the mental process of making connections to make sense of the world, which is just a bunch of electrochemical reactions. When one neuron fires, it doesn't mean anything, but when many fires simultaneously, it forms a thought. As the number of these firings goes up, ideas, concepts, and beliefs are formed. A belief is a thought that has been thought about more than once. Because of the patterns formed by associations, our beliefs affect how we react to stimuli or situations.

Emotions are the link between thoughts and how they shape reality. What you usually think affects how you feel, affecting what you do. This creates patterns that soon become your life's idea or accepted norm. When you believe in something, you subconsciously look for proof to back up your beliefs, and if you don't realize it, your life runs on auto-pilot until you figure out what's going on. You may believe that you are not smart, and every time you make a small mistake, you link it to the idea that you are not smart. This kind of connection is something you make with everything you see and hear, and it's the foundation of who you are. And there's nothing wrong with it, except for how you've been giving meaning to the things that have happened in your life, which is usually self-deprecating.

The Pygmalion effect is the idea that high expectations from others and an individual lead to good performance. In his 1969 article, J. Sterling Livingston writes that managers' and teachers' high expectations of their employees and students eventually come true. He also says that managers should pay extra attention to new employees and pair them with the right bosses to set the right expectations. This will set the groundwork for long-term productivity gains.

The well-known placebo effect proves that what we believe does change what happens to us. Ellen Langer, a psychologist at Harvard, did a study with hotel maids whose jobs required them to move around. She found that about 67% of these women thought they didn't get any exercise. Even though they worked out every day, their bodies didn't show any improvements. So, the person experimenting split the women into two groups. One group was told about the daily exercise requirements, while the other was not. The informed group had low blood pressure, lost weight, and had the right waist to hips ratio. In another case, a woman with nausea was given a powerful drug that was said to be magical and cure nausea. It did make her feel better, but the drug she was given, ipecac, is known to make people feel sick instead of making them feel better. Rather than the drug itself, it was the way it was presented to her by someone in a position of authority and the strong suggestion that it would make her feel better that caused biochemical reactions. So, we can say that what you think affects your experience.

The mind can't distinguish between what is real and what is made up. When you think about a certain stimulus, your brain forms the same pattern of nerve cells that it forms when you see it. Because of this, many teachings about the law of attraction are about imagining, visualizing, and feeling the emotions of having what you want. If you think about something enough, it becomes a belief, and by some mysterious force, it comes true.

If you can train your brain to think differently and

change your beliefs, you can have everything you want. When you are sure of something, like the woman who got rid of her sickness by taking a drug that made her sick, you expect it to happen. When you give something your attention, you make it more likely to happen in your life. For example, if you want to make more money, it makes sense to focus on opportunities that will help you do that. They say that energy flows where your attention goes. The great thing about this is that you can choose what to pay attention to. Reality can be changed, even though most people think life flows and things happen.

CHAPTER 1
MY LIFE PATH WITH THE POWER OF MY THOUGHTS

You've probably said, "I knew this was going to happen", more than once. Was it a sign, or did you think that way, and things turned out that way?

Consider a few events in your life and recall what you thought before they occurred. You might be surprised to find that many times there was a link between what you were thinking and what happened. You may find it difficult to believe, but your thoughts have power. The thoughts we think over and over affect how we react and feel, what we do and react, and our life and the people around us.

How we think determines how we live.

This means we should be careful with our thoughts, especially the ones we think repeatedly. One thought is insufficient to create a significant effect in our life. However, if we keep repeating the same concept, it will gather strength, strengthen, and affect our lives.

When we have the same thought repeatedly, it leaves a strong mark on our subconscious mind, which then works to make this thought come true in our lives. Thoughts are like movies we watch in our heads. If we keep watching the same movie in our minds, it will show up in our lives and become true.

How to Use Your Thoughts to Change Your Life

Your thoughts can shape your life, help you make changes, and improve things. You should stop thinking about what you don't want and start thinking about what you do want. It's like watching a new movie in your head that you like better than the one you're watching right now.

The new mental movie will change your actions, thoughts, and behavior over time. It will also bring people, situations, and events that match your new ideas into your life. But you should remember that a single thought isn't strong enough to change your life. If you keep thinking the same thing, it will get stronger over time and change your life.

When you have the same thought over and over, it takes root in your subconscious mind and starts to change your life and even the world around you. The nicest part about this strategy is that you don't have to put effort into making it work. You must choose the thoughts you want to manifest and repeat them in your head.

How to Use the energy and power of Your Thoughts

You want to change the fact that you are shy when you meet new people. Forcing yourself to talk to people doesn't always work, and it could make you feel awkward and act strange.

There is a better way for you to change the way you act. With the help of visualization, you can change how you act and do things. With the help of visualization techniques, you can change your life by using the great power of your thoughts.

How to Use Visualization to Change Habits

If you want to stop being timid, imagine yourself feeling confident and talking easily with others. This is like daydreaming, which is easy and fun and doesn't take much work. What you have to do is:

Imagine yourself being able to talk easily and confidently. Think about how easy it is for you to speak, how much you enjoy expressing yourself, and how everyone listens carefully to every word you say.

When you use this method, you make a picture in your mind of what you want to achieve.

Add details, colors, sounds, smells, and action to these mental scenes. If you say them often, believe in them and pay attention, your subconscious mind will help you make them come true naturally.

This way, you can:

- Get rid of bad habits and make new ones;

- Learn new skills and abilities;

- Change your situation;

- Get whatever you want.

You can get a new job, improve your relationships, make more money, or improve your life by using the power of your thoughts.

Changes like these don't happen all at once. They take

time and depend on how serious you are about your efforts and how much time and thought you put into your new thinking.

Even though this is mental work, you don't just sit back and wait for results. You should keep an open mind and be ready to act when necessary.

Decide what you want to get or accomplish, and then think about it often or at certain times throughout the day. These repeated thoughts would get stronger and, in the end, bring about the conditions and events that match your thinking.

Thoughts do have real power. You've probably done it a lot without even realizing it. But if you know how it works and how to use it on purpose, you can change, improve, and take charge of your life.

CHAPTER 2
WHAT ARE BELIEFS?

A person's belief is an idea that they think is true.

A person's belief can be based on things they know for sure, like mathematical principles, or on things they have faith in. A belief can come from many places, such as:

- The acceptance of cultural and societal norms (like religion);

- What other people say; (e.g. Education or mentoring).

A person's possible belief stays with them until they accept it as true and add it to their own set of beliefs. Each person looks at these possible beliefs and tries to find good reasons or proof. When someone accepts a belief as true and is willing to fight for it, we say it is part of their belief system.

What is a personal value?

Values are strong beliefs about what is important to a person that doesn't change over time. They become the rules people use to plan their lives and decide what to do. A person's belief will become valuable when they become more committed to it and see it as important.

Beliefs can be put into different values, such as those that have to do with happiness, money, success at work, or family. To make clear, rational, responsible, and consistent decisions, a person must be able to explain their values.

What is an attitude?

Attitudes are how people feel about others and the current situation before making decisions that lead to behavior. People's attitudes are mostly based on their core values and beliefs.

But things that a person may not have internalized as beliefs and values can still affect how they feel when deciding. The desire to please, being politically correct, convenience, peer pressure, and psychological stressors are all common influences.

If people haven't thought through what they believe and value, these influences are more likely to change their minds. This process includes thinking about the rules that could help them find common ground or decide which values are more important. Lack of self-awareness or critical insight, as well as ambivalence or uncertainty about values, can make it harder to make good decisions and lead to bad behavior.

CHAPTER 3
HOW DO BELIEFS ARISE?

What occurred to you when you were young, and your life experiences might shape your current self-perception and how you interpret the world around you. These things shape your core beliefs, which are usually universal and unchangeable. Parents, culture, and environments greatly impact how we think and believe from birth. Our thoughts, feelings, values, habits, and responses to stimuli are all based on our beliefs. One's first seven years are the most important. During these years, a child learns to see and understand the world. After seven years of age, life experiences change how the subconscious mind is set up. We get them from what other people say to us, what we hear on the news, what we read, and anything else that comes from the outside. Beliefs are not separate from each other. These beliefs talk to each other, change, and make up a system as a whole. As people grow and change, their belief systems change too. This is how people make sure they will live. Beliefs can tell us how to enjoy and live our lives, for better or worse. You learn these ideas as a child, and they stay with you (like glue!) as an adult.

How do these Beliefs Drive us?

There are two parts to our minds. The Mind of the Conscious and the Mind of the Subconscious. It has been found that 95% of how we react to the outside world, which our five senses pick up on, is controlled by our subconscious mind. Our conscious mind, which is in charge of logic, only plays a 5% role in processing stimuli and deciding how to respond or act. The beliefs we pick up throughout life shape this part of our minds. These beliefs make us feel, and when we feel, we act.

Tribalism and religious fundamentalism are deeply held beliefs that can lead to violent or crazy behavior. When people get stuck in their beliefs and don't question them now and then, the problem becomes dangerous. Our beliefs also lead us regarding our social and political lives. The approach of nonviolence advocated by Martin Luther King Jr. shifted the civil rights movement's focus and helped bring about the Civil Rights Act of 1968. People have school systems because they think that education can make people smarter. Let's use the fact that you just went through a break as an example. Your beliefs may have changed. After going through something painful, you might have different ideas about yourself and the world.

There are times when your feelings affect what you believe, but if they stay the same, you will likely be unable to have a satisfying relationship. You will get hurt by people who didn't do anything to you. It's important to remember that we don't want to permanently change how people see us for the worse. Always try to see things from a balanced point of view.

Humans' love can connect with God's love and rise to its level. Then you will be happier and more satisfied than someone with the first set.

Can we reprogram the Beliefs?

As we've already said, your core beliefs don't stand alone. Instead, they tend to work together and make each other stronger. If one belief changes, the whole system will change as well. If it is a core belief, changing could cause the system to break down. If a set of certain beliefs changes, other parts of the system will need to be moved around to make the system work again. Scientists have shown that when we change what we think or believe, we send our cells completely different messages and change how they act. Practicing mindfulness and gratitude can permanently change your cells from being pessimistic to being more optimistic. So, to improve your situation, you must change how you see "reality" by changing your beliefs. To change how our lives go, we must change how we think.

CHAPTER 4
HOW DO BELIEFS INFLUENCE OUR LIVES?

Here are three ways in which what you believe can change what you experience.

1. Your beliefs affect how you act.

Beliefs can change reality in a simple way that doesn't require quantum physics: they can change how people act. For example, if you think you're good enough to get your dream job and deserve it, you're probably more likely to notice and look for opportunities to help you get there. You also have a better chance of doing well in an interview. The common belief is that being too confident can backfire, but research shows that it may help: People who are too sure of themselves tend to look more socially skilled and higher on the social ladder, even if the people judging them know how good they are.

Beliefs can also affect how people treat their health.

Confidence in one's abilities has been shown to increase the likelihood that an individual will engage in healthful behaviors like diet and exercise. However, there is a limit to positivity: When people think negatively of themselves, such as when they worry they might be sick, they tend to take better care of their health, according to studies. Unaware of their dangers, people may not be motivated to make healthy decisions.

Strong convictions can be held regarding one's fundamental identity. While feelings of guilt (that you did something wrong) can motivate you to make amends, studies show that feelings of shame (that you are a bad person) can backfire and make it even less likely that you will make amends. Similarly, there is some proof that praising character rather than behavior is more effective in motivating good conduct. One study found that kids who were told they had a hand in doing a good deed (like sharing their marbles with less fortunate kids) went on to do even more acts of kindness than kids whose behavior was praised alone or not praised at all.

2. What you believe affects how other people act.

Your beliefs can change your reality by changing how

you act and how other people act, whether close friends or total strangers. In a well-known study, men were told that a woman they talked to on the phone was either attractive or not attractive. Outside observers listened to the recordings and found that as the conversation continued, the women who were seen as more attractive became friendlier and likelier than those who were seen as less attractive. This suggests that the participants' expectations affected how they saw their conversation partner and caused them to act in ways that confirmed their expectations. This has also been seen in several other situations, such as when teachers and students talk to each other.

Your beliefs may also make your romantic partner act similarly. Research shows that people who see their partners in a more idealized light than their partners see themselves are more likely to stay together, are happier with their relationships, and have less conflict over time. How could this be? One reason is that idealizers give their partners a sense of security and make them feel better about the relationship. In turn, partners who feel more secure are more likely to act in kind and helpful ways, which makes the relationship more satisfying. During a conflict, people who overestimate how hostile their partners are more likely to act in ways that make their partners even more hostile and reject them.

3. What you believe can affect how healthy you are.

Health and disease are affected by many different factors that interact with each other. Many of these factors are out of control, such as your genes, exposure to environmental toxins, history of trauma, and social and economic circumstances. But research shows that beliefs are also important. In one study, middle-aged adults who had more positive thoughts about getting older lived an average of 7.6 years longer than those who had more negative thoughts. This was true even when the participants' current health and other risk factors were considered. In several other studies, more optimistic people were found to be less likely to get heart disease, even when other risk factors were considered.

Research on the placebo effect also shows the link between beliefs and health. Even if a treatment is just a sugar pill, the fact that someone thinks it will work is sometimes enough to make it work. Even though the placebo effect is most often seen in subjective reports of symptoms, even when there are no physical changes to match, there is evidence for some objective, measurable effects: For example, placebos can change the way the brain responds to pain, and they have been shown to raise dopamine levels in people with Parkinson's disease, which can temporarily relieve symptoms.

How can you use your faith to make your life better? You can do things that change the way you usually think, like keeping a gratitude journal or learning to meditate. These habits can help you see and appreciate the good things in your life and stop you from getting stuck in negative, unhelpful thoughts. Second, you can make clear plans for how you want to go about each day and try to act in a way that fits those plans. Even when things don't go your way, you'll know that you're moving in the right direction and using the power you have.

CHAPTER 5
LIMITING BELIEFS AND HOW TO OVERCOME THEM

Have you ever thought, "I'm not good at this, so I should avoid doing it?" These beliefs are frequently based on negativity and fear, preventing us from experiencing new opportunities.

You are not alone if you have had similar thoughts. Many professionals, including entrepreneurs, struggle with self-limiting beliefs that stifle potential success. The key is to learn to recognize and overcome limiting beliefs.

Limiting beliefs in teamwork can impact everything from culture to overall performance to team efficiency. We've identified the top ten limiting beliefs people have and offered advice for combating them daily.

What exactly are limiting beliefs?

To put it simply, a limiting belief is an idea or thought process that you have about yourself that imposes restrictions. These convictions are often unfounded criticisms you level at yourself and can lead to undesirable outcomes.

A person's self-limiting beliefs can prevent them from taking advantage of opportunities to grow personally and professionally. For example, you may feel more vulnerable when public speaking is required. This is because of false assumptions about your communication skills.

The negative outlook that can result from holding onto limiting beliefs can have a devastating effect on your mental health and your great ability to take advantage of new possibilities and life experiences. That's why it's important to become aware of one's biases and cultivate feelings of self-worth. Any time you let your biases about other people get in the way of working together, the quality of your job suffers.

The effects of self-limiting beliefs

The destructive effects of limiting beliefs and negative thinking on workplace innovation and morale cannot be overstated. Let's say you're developing a new procedure but are too timid to suggest an improved approach.

Almost sure the outcome will not be original.

If you're in a leadership role, addressing the limiting beliefs of your team members is a key to unleashing their creativity and motivation. By refusing to let go of such preconceived notions, people limit their creativity and ability to contribute to society. Not coming up with new approaches is the biggest roadblock to team success.

It is during these daring moments that true growth occurs, and each team member must believe in themselves enough to push past boundaries. That is why it is critical to promote positive thinking to empower your team to do and be their best.

Ten examples of common limiting beliefs

Limiting beliefs are any self-deprecating thoughts that prevent you from growing as an individual. Learning the most common limiting beliefs, from verbal beliefs to body language and defense mechanisms, can help you identify them if they arise.

Here are ten common examples of some limiting beliefs to recognize and correct in the workplace to work on self-improvement:

- I'm not qualified: "I'm not qualified to manage this project."

- I'm too old or young to be a manager: "I'm too young to be a manager."

- I don't have time to invest in myself: "I don't have time to invest in myself."

- I'm not intelligent enough: "I'm not intelligent enough to lead this meeting."

- I lack experience: "I lack experience for this significant career change."

- I'll never be successful: "In my industry, I'll never be successful."

- I'm not wealthy: "I'm not wealthy enough to enjoy my life."

- I'll never be among the best: "I'll never be among the team's best."

- I'm not talented: "I'm not talented enough to advance."

- I can never be a great leader: "With the lack of confidence, I'll never be a great leader."

These kinds of beliefs stem from fear, and everyone has them. The goal is to learn how to recognize and combat limiting beliefs, so they do not keep you from venturing outside your comfort zone.

You may be tempted to tell yourself that you're not great enough or that you'll never be good enough to keep yourself safe, but these beliefs ultimately prevent you from empowering yourself and your team to be the best.

The trick is to be aware of your own limiting beliefs and use that awareness to reframe how you think about yourself. You can also improve your team management abilities by encouraging others to do the same.

What factors contribute to limiting beliefs?

Your brain's attempt to protect you from further pain is the root cause of limiting beliefs, fueled by many different things. Triggers include things like fears, imposter syndrome, and traumatic experiences.

These self-defeating ideas typically form at a formative age, then shift and reshape as you gain exposure to new information and perspectives. Whether you've had a traumatic experience that has left you fearful of repeat encounters or the future, limiting beliefs can prevent you from developing more optimistic ones.

Finding out where your self-limiting ideas came from is a great first step toward changing your worldview. But there are other ways to conquer your fears in the workplace.

How to Overcome Your Limiting Beliefs

Overcoming limiting beliefs is difficult, especially if you are unaware of them. But did the examples of limiting beliefs I provided make you aware of the beliefs holding you back? You must first identify the limiting belief. Recognize and accept it.

Then you must discover the lie because a limiting belief is not entirely true. For example, perhaps your mother died in a car accident, and you believe you cannot drive.

But you can because you took driving lessons and had a driver's license. You can drive but don't because you tell yourself, "You can't."

The next step is to discuss it. You may require professional assistance when your limiting belief becomes ingrained in your identity. However, if your limiting belief is simply an excuse to avoid doing something, you should just do it.

Reframe your beliefs, put what you think you can't do to the test, and see what happens. Continue to practice breaking old, bad habits, developing a growth mindset, and believing in yourself - with no limits this time!

Other strategies that can help you overcome your limiting beliefs include:

- Try meditation

- Positive affirmations

- Vision boards

- Positive self-talk

- Journaling for self-growth

- Minimalism

- Experiment with new things, become curious, and explore

CHAPTER 6
POSITIVE BELIEFS TO BOOST YOUR SELF-ESTEEM

Beliefs, like words, have tremendous power. What you tell yourself in your head significantly impacts your self-image and self-esteem. That is because negative self-talk is accompanied by negative beliefs about yourself, the world, and others, fueling a pessimistic, weak, and unfavorable outlook. Beliefs are so powerful that they can lead you to a reality you have created solely through thought. So, if you don't think you're fit enough to run for more than 5 minutes, you won't.

Similarly, if you decide you can do it rationally and emotionally, you will. When I say "emotionally," I mean with your entire being, that is, your mind and body. In The Biology of Belief, Lipton (2015) explains that "thoughts, the mind's energy, directly influence how the physical brain controls the body's physiology." That would explain why there are so many stories of people defying terminal cancer diagnoses, for example, and living much longer lives. Below are five positive beliefs to boost self-esteem to help you start thinking and feeling better about yourself:

1- I am significant.

You are significant to others even if you are not currently in a relationship or have many friends. You matter as a living being to the universe and yourself and others around you, even if they don't know you. Life is valuable, and we all want to protect it. As a result, even though I have never met you, I wish you the best as a fellow human being. And, no, you don't have to be a therapist or a monk to think this way, as many people do.

2- I am capable.

Do you know how many skills you need to read this blog post? Even if you are depressed, in despair, or heartbroken, you can wake up every day and face your fears. Being human can be difficult at times, but we learn to control our lives from a young age. Remind yourself that it is the effort that counts, not the outcome. Every attempt demonstrates to yourself, the world, and others that you are alive and connected.

3- You can take it.

You have overcome illness, inclement weather, adversity, and disappointment. You've been able to get up and get things done even when you wanted to curl up and disappear. You showed up even when your body was weak. When you couldn't be there for yourself, you were there for others. You felt isolated and resentful, but you tried to be civil and respectful to others. You dealt with your losses as best you could, despite the lack of validation or support from others. You are tough and can withstand pain and discomfort.

4- I have faith in others.

Would you have gotten this far without the assistance of others? Even though some of us are quite independent, we all survive and thrive because we work together. Relationships of all kinds are dangerous because everyone enters them with expectations, vulnerabilities, and at least one trauma. We all get hurt at some point because we are flawed beings. The good news is that, as previously stated, you can handle it! If you are disappointed, as with most things in life, you will eventually get over it.

5- I am competent.

You were good enough to enter this world. Regardless of the circumstances, you were capable of growth and development. You were talented enough to reach your age and know the people you do. You were good enough to accomplish what you did and make something of it. You are worthy of being alive and every breath you take. You are sufficient and deserving of everything you still have to offer yourself, the universe, and others. You are sufficient because you are yourself, and you are unique.

If you struggle to feel whole and happy because of low self-esteem, it is time to tell your brain a different story about yourself, the world, and those around you. I strongly advise you to write down the above beliefs and incorporate them into your meditation practice. Create imaginary scenarios where you see yourself acting as described above once you have reached a calm state of mind and feel at one with your body. Connect with the positive bodily sensations evoked by these images as if you were right there, enjoying this new way of being.

Repeat the exercise daily to see how it affects your emotional health.

CHAPTER 7
HOW DO I CHANGE MY BELIEFS?

I'm either too old or too young to do that."

"I intend to spend my life alone."

"I'll never find a job that makes me happy. It's only a job."

"That is something I will never be able to do."

Limiting beliefs are expressed in these phrases. They are horrible and are an excuse for not achieving your goals.

Limiting beliefs keep us in our familiar surroundings. They can severely limit our personal and professional development and achievement. We regard these thoughts, whether conscious or unconscious, as absolute truths. However, these negative thoughts, which impede our progress toward our life goals, can be overcome and replaced with positive messages. You can change everything by changing your thinking.

Why do we hold such limiting beliefs?

Most limiting beliefs are unconscious thoughts that appear as defense mechanisms to avoid potential frustrations, failure, and disappointment. You may have been hurt by something in the past, and now, when you're in a similar situation, your mind finds a specific way to try to block it out. A good way to start fighting against limiting beliefs is to figure out where they come from by determining what makes you feel bad. These limiting thoughts and beliefs can stem from a variety of sources, including:

- Personal beliefs are the experiences a person has had that have led to the development of certain blocks.

- Hereditary experiences and beliefs related to how we were created, the ideas and behaviors we observe and reinforce throughout our lives.

- Fear or excuse refers to anything you use to avoid doing something specific or to refrain from taking action because you are afraid of failing.

- Social circles of those around you and those with influence over you.

- Society can impose standards that lead to limiting beliefs.

- Religious beliefs can sometimes spread limiting thoughts because their preaching usually defines which attitudes are acceptable in the eyes of the divinity in which a person believes.

Consider what you want to accomplish but aren't working on to identify your limiting beliefs. Then look for the justification you discovered for not doing the thing in question. This justification is usually found in the sentence's "why." Trying to untangle such limiting beliefs is easier said than done. Speaking with trusted friends, family, or mentors can be beneficial in this situation.

So, how do you get past your limiting beliefs?

Below are some ways you can change your beliefs.

1. Recognize one of your limiting beliefs.

The first step toward overcoming your limiting beliefs is to identify them. If you are concerned that there may be multiple limitations, begin with the largest one and then repeat with each limiting belief.

2. Accept that it is only a belief.

Recognize that your belief may be based on false assumptions. It is likely false and merely a belief, not a fact.

3. Examine your own beliefs

Question your belief now that you've realized it's just a belief rather than a fact. Put it to the test by asking questions like:

- Is this belief supported by evidence? What facts back up your claim?

- Have I always thought this way? What, if anything, has changed?

- Is there evidence to contradict my belief?

- What would it be like to consider the opposites of my beliefs?

- Is this belief assisting me in reaching my objectives?

- How would I consider this belief if I were someone else (for example, Albert Einstein, Oprah Winfrey, Steve Jobs, an entrepreneur, a doctor, and so on)?

Many of these questions may appear strange, but they are intended to broaden your understanding of the subject. It trains you to think "outside the box." When arguing against your initial thinking, you may realize that it is not exactly what you were thinking, prompting you to shift your paradigm to something more positive and encouraging.

4. Be aware of the potentially negative consequences

What are the ramifications of holding onto your limiting belief? Holding on to the belief that you cannot pass a selection because you failed on the first attempt can prevent you from passing and living a better life in the future.

5. Develop a new belief

Choose something new to believe in that will help you improve your life. This transition may be difficult. Depending on how long you have thought about and lived through what led you to believe what you believe, it may have created a strong emotional bond firmly rooted in the belief. If you want to change, you must have the strength and courage to change your thinking and adopt new beliefs.

6. Put it into action.

Take action and begin putting things in place that support your new belief. If your limiting belief was that you were "too old to start exercising," start by adopting an "It will never be too late to start again" belief and then go for a 15-minute walk today to start exercising and creating a habit from there.

Conditioning yourself to your new beliefs entails imagining the reality you want for yourself and visualizing the outcomes you desire. Visualization is an excellent method for building anticipation. You will mentally experience the desired outcome. This will send congruent signals to your brain, causing it to work for you.

What role does mentoring play in the process of overcoming limiting beliefs?

In addition to the steps outlined above, mentoring and coaching can be extremely beneficial in identifying and overcoming limiting beliefs.

This methodology employs several techniques in the pursuit of personal development. Part of that process includes self-discovery (in coaching), motivation, and learning and understanding from those who have achieved success (in mentoring).

When you realize that you can change your life completely by changing your certain beliefs, you will discover that you can eliminate toxic thoughts that previously kept you from achieving your goals. When a coach or mentor focuses on your skills and how they can improve, you will be encouraged to overcome limiting beliefs and achieve your objectives.

CHAPTER 8
MY BELIEFS AND VALUES

Would you rather own a beautiful home or travel the world for a year? Do you have a consistent income or a flexible schedule? Should you save for retirement or splurge on an expensive gift? The answer was obvious for many of you, but your answer is dependent on your values and beliefs.

If you value security and stability, splurges or a year of travel may not appeal to you as much as someone who values variety. That is how your values and beliefs influence your decisions and how your decisions shape your life. So, what is the distinction between values and beliefs? Once you understand the distinction, you can use it to live a more fulfilling life.

Beliefs vs values

While we frequently use the terms interchangeably, there are significant differences between values and beliefs. Your values are the principles by which you live. They are your standards for what is good, fair, and meaningful. They influence what you seek and avoid, what you enjoy, and what you find draining.

Your values have a direct impact on your actions. They influence your daily behavior and character and are related to your needs. What you value is whatever you feel is missing from your life or is most important to you. These things make us feel more fulfilled and at ease.

Your beliefs, on the other hand, are truths that you accept without question. They develop over time and are influenced by your upbringing, positive and negative events in your life, the breadth and depth of your knowledge, the past outcomes of your decisions, and the imagined plan for the future.

Beliefs are broad generalizations that influence your morals or values and are usually related to any religion or culture in any area. They are a certain acceptance that something is true or exists, even without concrete proof. These worldview assumptions stem from a variety of sources.

Your values are underpinned and influenced by your beliefs. You may believe that contributing something unique and different will leave your imprint on the world. Creativity is the value that corresponds to that belief. Friendships and connections may be more important to you than anything else. Loyalty is the underlying value there.

One thing that can get lost in the debate over values vs beliefs is that they are not always healthy. Many of us unconsciously developed limiting beliefs during childhood and adulthood. Limiting beliefs are thoughts that don't represent your true values, such as "I don't deserve love" or "I'll never be good enough." You must bring these negative thoughts to the surface and replace them with empowering ones that reflect your true beliefs and values.

Values and beliefs list

Are you unsure of your values and beliefs? You're not by yourself. Many people go through life without ever determining what is important to them. One of the reasons people become distracted by power or wealth is because of this. They lose sight of what is truly important. We never discover why we are the way we are and instead pursue someone else's definition of success.

If you need some assistance determining your core values, start with this list of values and beliefs:

- **Appreciation:** Do you like being acknowledged by others and validating those you care about?

- **Creativity:** How important is imagination and creating new ideas or projects?

- **Generosity:** If you truly believe that the key to living is to give, then generosity is undoubtedly one of your values.

- **Self-reliance:** Those who value self-reliance prioritize independence and not relying on others.

- **Integrity:** How do you react when someone lies to you or refuses to take responsibility for their actions?

- **Authenticity:** Being yourself means not being swayed by the certain opinions of others, which is essential for those who value authenticity.

- **Loyalty:** If you keep your promises and always have your friends' and partners' backs, you are likely a loyal person.

- **Compassion:** Do you listen well? Do your friends seek your advice?

- **Positivity:** Those who value positivity exhibit gratitude and optimism.

- **Courage:** Those who stand up for what is right and believe in what they stand for value courage.

- **Resilience:** If you take pride in your inner strength and ability to overcome obstacles, you value resilience.

How to live following your beliefs and values

Knowing the difference between values and beliefs and identifying your core values is essential for living a meaningful and passionate life. Life becomes more meaningful when you stop making decisions based on what others think and start making decisions based on your priorities.

APPRECIATE YOUR THOUGHTS

"Your values and beliefs control every decision in your life," Tony Robbins says. Recognizing the power of your beliefs is the first step in creating the life you want. You must recognize that your beliefs influence your decisions, actions, and destiny. Determine whether your current belief systems are positive or negative. Are they constructive or destructive?

Others' influence results in negative and destructive beliefs. When you become aware of these negative beliefs, you can reshape them into empowering ones that serve you. Allow them to reflect your true values rather than those imposed by others. You can also reinforce the positive beliefs you already have.

DISCOVER YOUR DIRECTING PRINCIPLES

Understanding what motivates you is the starting point for using your values to guide your decisions. What motivates you to act? What motivates you to achieve your objectives? Do you prefer excitement or stability? Do you prefer pleasure over pain? What gets you out of bed feeling energized and joyful in the morning?

Investigating these unseen influences can reshape their hold on your life. This will assist you in resetting your intentions toward success and joy rather than misery and suffering, allowing you to live a more fulfilling and successful life. It's up to you to shift your attention to your most important beliefs and values because, as an expert says, "what you value determines what you focus on."

THINK ABOUT HOW YOUR THOUGHTS AFFECT YOUR RELATIONSHIPS.

Your personal beliefs and values significantly impact how you create and maintain healthy relationships. Relationships can bring a lot of joy and love, but they can also bring a lot of disappointment and sadness. When you enter a relationship, your limiting beliefs about yourself and others are amplified, which means your values are also amplified. When two partners argue about values and beliefs, or when beliefs prevent them from finding a genuine connection, the relationship is unlikely to last. Finding someone who shares your values and beliefs is the first step toward a stronger relationship.

Values such as significance and appreciation can harm relationships. If you are drawn to conflict in a relationship as a validator of attention, you will seek that sense of significance in harmful and dangerous ways. It's difficult to admit when your values aren't serving you. Still, if you recognize the pattern and shift your mind to believe that relationships must be positive and loving, you'll notice that in your relationships with others.

CREATE NEW BELIEFS AND VALUES

"What you consistently hold in your mind is what you will experience in your life," says Tony Robbins. Now that you've recognized that your values and beliefs guide you use your power to change them. When your beliefs align with your true self, you can make new ground rules for yourself.

It's time to imagine a life you're insanely excited about. A life that would exceed your wildest expectations. A life that is only possible by reevaluating your current value system. Recognize how your beliefs influence your values. Then devise a personalized life plan to achieve it. Include your new life mission/purpose and a list of values and beliefs to help you achieve it. You will then be able to set new goals for yourself.

You should now have an evident picture of your beliefs and values. You know how you want your life to be. You understand that every thought and action you take throughout the day leads you to your destiny and creates an extraordinary life. You understand how to control your beliefs rather than allowing them to control you. By rethinking your approach to values and decision-making, you'll be better equipped to create the life you want.

CHAPTER 9
THE RICH VS POOR BELIEF

What is the distinction between rich and poor beliefs? What distinguishes the successful from the rest of us? Many people do not achieve financial freedom because they lack one thing: proper belief. Everything begins with how you perceive money, wealth, and success. It is not due to chance, birth, or connections.

The biggest differences between them can be found in what they think, how they act, and what they believe. Rich and poor think and act differently based on how much money they have. Rich people think differently than poor people and people in the middle class.

They have different perspectives on money, wealth, themselves, other people, and life. As a result, you will have some alternative beliefs to choose from in your mind. This way, you can catch yourself thinking like a poor person and quickly switch to thinking like a rich person.

A positive attitude, a focus on doing the right thing over doing the best, becoming a lifelong learner, and specific risk management techniques are all differences between the rich and the poor. This lowers their chances of becoming impoverished after a disaster and helps them achieve their financial goals in the long run.

A wealthy belief will tell you to be self-sufficient and to create multiple income streams. It will advise you to assemble a team of smarter people than you to maximize the efforts of talented individuals. The main reason "the rich get richer while the poor get poorer" is because of what the rich believe. Bill Gates said, "It would be easy for us to fall behind and become a mediocre company if we didn't keep hiring great people and moving forward at full speed."

So, which of these beliefs do you hold? Let's look at twelve startling differences in how rich and poor or middle-class people think.

1. Wealthy People Believe "I Create My Own Life."

Poor beliefs hold that "Life just happens to me." If you

want to create wealth, you must believe that you are in control of your life and create every moment, especially your financial life.

Instead of accepting responsibility for their circumstances, poor people prefer to play the victim. Of course, the dominant thought process of any "victim" is "poor me." And presto, by the law of intention, that's exactly what they get: "poor," as in money, me.

2. Rich vs Poor Belief: Rich Win the Money Game

Poor beliefs play the money game to avoid losing. Poor people prefer to play defense rather than offence in the money game. Let me ask you this: What are your chances of winning if you were to play any sport or game solely on defense? The majority of people agree on slim and none.

Yet, that is exactly how most people approach money. They are more concerned with survival and security than with wealth and abundance. So, what is your objective? What is your true goal? What is your true goal?

The ultimate goal of the wealthy is to amass enormous wealth and abundance. Poor people's main goal is to have "enough to pay my bills." If they could do that on time, it would be a miracle. Let me tell you again how powerful your thoughts are. When your goal is to have just enough money to pay your bills, you'll get just enough money to pay your bills and usually nothing more. What you want is what you get.

3. Rich Beliefs Are Dedicated to Financial Success

Poor beliefs make it difficult to achieve wealth. Most of us can think of good reasons why it would be great to be rich, but what about the other side? Is there anything about being rich or getting rich that might not be great?

Each of us has a wealth file in our heads. This file contains our personal beliefs about why being wealthy would be fantastic. However, for many people, their file also includes information on why being wealthy may not be so great. These people have conflicting internal messages about money, particularly wealth. The reason why most people never become wealthy is that they receive mixed messages.

Most people don't get what they want because they don't know what they want. Rich people are unequivocal in their desire for wealth. They are steadfast in their desire. They are completely committed to generating wealth. They are willing to do "whatever it will take" to obtain wealth as long as it is moral and ethical. Rich people do not send contradictory signals to the universe. People in poverty do.

I'm sorry that becoming wealthy is not a "walk in the park." It requires concentration, expertise, 100% effort, and "never say die" perseverance. You must make a conscious and subconscious commitment to it. You should believe that you can do it and deserve it. You are unlikely to succeed if you are not fully committed to creating wealth.

4. Rich vs Poor Belief: Rich People Have Big Ideas

Poor people have small minds. We once had a trainer teach at one of our seminars who went from having a net worth of $260 thousand to over $700 million in only three years. When asked what his secret was, he replied, "Everything changed the day I started thinking big."

Another specific way to think about it is to answer the following question: How many individuals do you serve or have an impact on?

In my business, for example, some trainers prefer to speak to groups of 20, others prefer groups of 100, others prefer an audience of 500, and still, others prefer audiences of 5000 or more. Is there a wage disparity between these trainers? Yes, there is.

- What is your name? What kind of dream life do you want to live?

- How would you like to play the game?

- Do you want to play in the majors, the big or the little leagues?

- Will you go big or go home? It's entirely up to you.

But listen to this. It isn't about you. It's all about carrying out your mission. It is about living your purpose. It's about contributing your piece to the world's puzzle. It's all about helping others.

Most of us are so focused on "me, me, and more me" that everything revolves around us. But, once again, it's not really about you; it's about adding value to the lives of others. It's entirely up to you. One path leads to poverty and misery, while the other leads to wealth, meaning, and fulfilment.

It's time to stop hiding and start walking around. It is time to stop needing and begin leading. It's time to start acting like the star you are.

5. Rich People's Beliefs Are Greater Than Their Problems

Poor people are dwarfed by their problems. It is not easy to become wealthy. It's a difficult journey with many twists and turns. The simple truth is that success is messy. The road is fraught with hazards, so most people avoid it. They don't want the issues.

This is the significant difference between rich and poor people. Rich and successful people are larger than their problems, whereas poor and unsuccessful people are smaller.

Poor people will go to almost any length to avoid anything that appears to be a problem. They shy away from difficulties. The irony is that in trying to avoid problems, they've ended up with the worst ones: they're broke and unhappy.

Instead of avoiding or getting rid of problems, the key to success is growing so that you are bigger than them.

It's just like getting dressed or brushing your teeth—nothing ordinary. No matter how much wealth you have or how big or small you play, you will still have problems. There will always be "problems" as long as you are still alive.

It's important to know that the size of any problem is never the real problem. What counts is how big you are!

Remember that you are the only one who can make your money grow. The goal is to improve yourself to the point where you can get past problems that stop you from making money and keep it once you have it.

Rich people do not shy away from problems, avoid problems, or complain about them. Rich people are financial warriors, and when faced with a challenge, they exclaim, "BRING IT ON!"

6. Rich vs Poor Belief: Rich People Concentrate on Possibilities

Poor people are preoccupied with problems. Rich people see opportunities in every situation and work hard to pursue them.

Rich beliefs anticipate potential growth. Poor beliefs result in potential loss. Rich beliefs are centered on rewards. Poor beliefs concentrate on the dangers.

We're not just talking about "positive thinking." We're talking about a way of looking at the whole world that you always do. Fear is what makes people poor. Their minds always look for what's wrong or what could go wrong. Their main thought is, "What if it doesn't work?" or, more directly, "It won't work." As we've already discussed, rich people take charge of their lives and think, "It will work because I will make it work."

In the financial world, as in most others, the risk is directly related to the reward. In general, the bigger the reward, the bigger the risk. People who think of themselves as wealthy are willing to take that risk. They try to take advantage of opportunities even when they don't have the skills to do so.

People with money expect to do well. They believe in their skills and creativity and know that if things go wrong, they can always make their money back or find another way to succeed. They look for ways to learn more to do the job better.

While the poor expect to fail. They don't believe in themselves or their abilities and think that failing would be terrible.

You must do something, buy anything, or start something to make money. Instead of looking for ways to lose money, you should look for ways to make money everywhere you go.

7. Rich Beliefs Always Place Emphasis on a Positive Attitude

Poor people do not have a positive attitude. Poor is a perception. It is a lack of optimism.

Dave Ramsey, a national best-selling author, once stated that the difference between being broke and being poor is attitude. The broke have no money now, but they have a positive attitude; they believe they can do better when they work toward doing better. They believe they will always be poor. The little man is unable to advance. The wealthy oppress the poor.

They can't save wealth because they think it will be

taken away, and they spend money they save or get as a bonus on pleasures because they don't think they could do better by doing something else. For example, if you believe you can't do better, you won't finish that difficult degree program or work a second job to get out of debt because it's pointless.

Or they believe they can't be wealthy because they believe the myth that most millionaires inherited their wealth and social standing. In reality, 80 per cent of the wealthy are the first generation, with less than 3 per cent inheriting enough to become millionaires.

A negative attitude can hamper even those with a good income. One classic example is being afraid to invest, so you keep your money in savings and earn less than the inflation rate. Another is that they consider money immoral, so they donate it to charities and "needy" friends and family.

They have nothing, so they have no savings for emergencies or retirement. This is why long-term financial success necessitates a positive mindset. Setbacks such as job loss or massive medical bills are viewed as temporary and worked through.

8. Rich Beliefs Do Not Display Their Wealth

People who have strong beliefs live frugal lives. The general public believes that the wealthy flaunt their wealth. We are duped when we see "the rich" wearing designer clothes, going on extravagant vacations, and throwing lavish parties. In reality, only a small number of truly wealthy people live this way, and most of those who do are high-income earners with little or no savings.

Once the money from a signing bonus or a record deal is gone, they have nothing left. Unfortunately, marketing campaigns that say you have to spend money in this way to get rich only add to this idea. But you can't do that if you spend money on flashy cars, expensive trips, and other signs of success.

The $500 car payment you make monthly, and the biggest house you can afford will keep you from getting rich. Most real millionaires live in homes they can afford and put paying off their mortgage at the top of their list. Even if they buy a used car and keep it running for ten years, they don't make car payments because they keep their cars for a long time.

As they build their businesses and portfolios, they are happy with how things are going. They earn their money by working hard. There is a widespread misconception that most millionaires are liars and cheaters. One myth is that the wealthy do not pay taxes, even though the top 1% pays 40% of all taxes.

Another myth is that the wealthy are dishonest con artists who made their fortune by exploiting others. In reality, surveys show that the most important trait that millionaire's value is integrity. You can't stay in business if you're constantly being sued for fraud or scamming customers. You can't build a business network or create quality relationships if you're a liar or a cheat.

9. Rich Beliefs Recognize the Importance of Education

Poor beliefs are blind to the significance of continuous learning or education. Rich beliefs continue to learn and improve their skills throughout their lives.

Education is still a major predictor of lifetime earnings. It should be noted that this does not imply that you must attend an expensive private college or obtain an advanced degree. However, you will certainly be poor if you do not complete high school.

One distinction between rich and poor beliefs is that the rich recognize the value of knowledge. They are not among the 40% of adults who do not read a book after finishing high school. They read industry publications to learn more about their field and perform better at work.

They're learning about money management and personal development to succeed in life. They are always learning. They will ensure that their certifications are maintained and seek additional certifications to qualify for raises and promotions.

10. Rich Beliefs Perform Better in Risk Management

Poor beliefs are frequently associated with apprehension about taking new risks.

The wealthy do not gamble with their money by going to casinos or investing in penny stocks. They take precautions to minimize risk. One way they accomplish this is by having adequate insurance coverage. They have life, health, and disability insurance to protect themselves and their families in a disaster. They will not start a business or invest without first analyzing its profitability.

They have an emergency fund with several months of savings to cover a major unexpected expense without going into debt. They prioritize self-protection over spending money on wants. This is not to say that they do not invest in stocks or real estate. It means they do their research before investing their money.

Before they buy, they research the properties and the costs to rehab and sell them. They do their homework before investing in stocks or mutual funds. Educating themselves on various topics lowers their risk level. As a result, one of the differences between rich and poor beliefs is that the poor frequently live in fear of disaster, whereas the rich expect to be able to weather the storm.

11. Rich vs Poor Belief: Rich People Create Multiple Income Streams

Poor people only have one source of income: their job. Poor people put all their eggs in one basket by relying on a single source of income.

The wealthy are known for their work ethic, but many

people work hard but remain impoverished. The wealthy operate in a variety of ways. One example is that they spend time planning their financial future. They save for retirement to have a passive source of income when they retire from their jobs.

They aggressively pay down debt and avoid incurring new debt to maximize their income. They devote time to managing their investments and make monthly investments, whether in a 401K or rental properties. If they own a business, they use it to supplement their income.

To generate additional revenue, it may be necessary to license intellectual property or rent out one of the suites. They may have a day job but teach or consult to supplement their income. This can also be considered risk management because it gives them a head start if they lose their job or want to start their own full-time business.

12. Rich Beliefs Believe in the power of saving, investing, and multiplying

Poor beliefs spend money on materialistic items. Poor people have no savings to invest in.

Rich people believe in saving, saving, saving. They save 10% to 20% of their net income every year. The wealthy are deliberate. They do not delay saving for the future. They begin saving with every paycheck and choose not to splurge to make the next 15% contribution to retirement.

They don't say anything about paying off the debt later. They devise a debt-reduction strategy and stick to it month after month until they are debt-free. According to "The Millionaire Next Door" and Chris Hogan's follow-up book "Everyday Millionaires," most millionaires by net worth either stick to a budget or send a set percentage of their income to savings and live off the rest.

In a nutshell, they make plans and stick to them. They set goals and usually achieve them by focusing on them and constantly working toward them. It's worth noting that it's not just about money. This is also why the wealthy are less likely to be obese. If you're already used to working toward financial goals regularly, an exercise and diet plan is just another plan to follow.

CHAPTER 9
PARENTS' BELIEFS

Parental motivational beliefs include role construction, school valence, and parental self-efficacy. The current study also looked at how these factors influenced parental involvement behaviors like home-based and school-based involvement. Parents install core beliefs and values in their children, which schools, churches, businesses, and the government reinforce. Secondary beliefs and values are more malleable. Believing in marriage is a fundamental belief; believing that people should marry young is a secondary belief. Marketers can influence secondary values but have little influence over core values.

CHAPTER 10

INNER CHILD WORK: HEAL BY REPARENTING YOURSELF

At first, becoming your parent may seem a little far-fetched. But what if working with your inner child is necessary for emotional healing?

You may consider yourself an adult simply because you have reached a certain age. The truth is that many adults harbor wounded children within them. We don't always notice it. We mask childhood trauma by staying busy and taking everything seriously.

Meanwhile, your inner child is the key to unending happiness, freedom, and creativity. It may be necessary to reparent yourself to gain access to these. Your inner child requires your acknowledgement and processing of its painful experiences.

Different people deal with childhood trauma in different ways. Some people may have it because they were abused badly as kids. Others are left out or ignored by their parents in more subtle ways, or they just can't fit in with their peers.

No matter what kind of trauma you've been through, working with your inner child can help you get better. This work is less about going "back in time" and more about going "inside." Michael Brown, who wrote The Presence Process, says:

"The past is no longer something "behind us" that we can "return" to. The past is over with. On the other hand, these unprocessed emotional charges stay with us as energetic conditions imprinted in our emotional body. We are basically "going in" instead of "going back." "All the answers are now inside of us."

Your inner child is always with you and ready to help you figure things out. Will you listen to what it says and let it lead you?

What Is Inner Child Work?

Jungian therapy is where the term "inner child" comes from. Carl Jung said that the "Child archetype" is the first step in becoming an individual or forming oneself.

Inner child work is now a common part of many types

of therapy, like Transactional Analysis and Gestalt. Working with your inner child is based on the fact that everyone was once a child. Those parts of us that were children don't just disappear as we get older.

In your unconscious mind, your childhood self still lives on. It shows how you were and what you were like when you were young. Think of it as one of your "subpersonalities" or parts of being human.

When you face problems that remind you of something bad that happened to you, your inner child is often brought out. Your child self is in charge until you process and integrate your memories of when you were a child.

"The inner child is a reflection of both the "negative" and "positive" parts of the child we used to be," says the definition. Unmet needs make children hide their feelings, and we still have children's innocence, creativity, and joy. This indicates that inner child work (also known as self-reparation) has two components.

The first is about reclaiming all of the positive characteristics of the child within. It's becoming playful and joyful for no apparent reason. It's cracking silly jokes and having a good time with your children, carefree and in the moment.

This aspect of inner child work is about freely expressing yourself. However, most people must also deal with their inner child's suppressed memories.

This is the second, and often more difficult, aspect of reparenting yourself. It's similar to what some call "shadow work." In a nutshell, it involves consciously processing painful feelings and experiences you have suppressed for a long time. This can be overwhelming, especially for those who were not provided necessities as children.

Richard Barrett explains in his theory of psychological development that as we enter the human experience, we all require two things before anything else. These are examples of physical safety and a specific sense of acceptance and belonging. If your parents or caregivers fail to meet these needs, they may follow you throughout your life.

You can meet those needs as an adult by reparenting

yourself. This is about becoming the exact type of parent your inner child requires. "But this isn't me!" you may think. I had a good childhood. My parents never abused me. They were crazy about me. We always had enough food and a safe place to live."

The tricky part is that your parents didn't have to do anything particularly bad to leave an impression on your child self. Childhood trauma can have its roots in the most seemingly innocent family dynamics.

For adults, it's just another day of balancing work, family, and social life. It could be the day that the child gets hurt badly. Then, they might carry those wounds into adulthood and pass them on to their children without knowing it.

Childhood Trauma And How It Happens

The word "trauma" conjures up images of horror. However, you do not have to have experienced severe childhood abuse to become traumatized.

A child's psyche is so fragile that even minor events can have a negative impact. Everything appears different in the eyes of a child. Because children completely rely on their caregivers to meet their needs, minor negligence can be interpreted as a huge threat.

Furthermore, children are unable to recognize their limited perspective. Everything they see, they believe. Their interpretation of life becomes their reality almost immediately.

Let me provide an example. I recently discussed our family relationships with my mother. We also discussed childhood trauma and inner child work. She asked if I wanted to know anything about my childhood, and she told me about hers. I inquired about a potentially traumatic event that I am unlikely to recall.

She stated unequivocally that something had stayed with her until today. My father drove my mother and me to Grandma's house for a few weeks when I was about ten months old. He then returned to work.

When he finally returned, I was lying on the bed while my mother dressed me. I turned to face him at that precise moment. My mother swears I recognized him and became upset that he had abandoned us for so long.

I burst into tears. I sobbed and sobbed some more. I

didn't want him to have me for hours on end.

I'm not sure if that particular incident traumatized me. I do know that I struggle with abandonment issues as an adult. When I first entered a romantic relationship, I was terrified of rejection.

We're often taught as children to hide our pain when we go through such traumatic experiences. Many parents discourage their children from crying or expressing their anger. Only when we are cheerful, smiling, and polite are we told we are "good."

Childhood trauma becomes unconscious in this way. If you keep it hidden from others long enough, you'll eventually start hiding it from yourself. You can deceive yourself into thinking you've "overcome it" this way.

In reality, the wounded child within you continues to run your life. It forces you to engage in behaviors that undermine your happiness without your knowledge. This usually continues until the problem is addressed through inner child work.

All this talk about childhood trauma isn't meant to point the finger at your parents — or anyone else who has caused you pain. These people were most likely doing their best with what they had and knew.

However, due to their circumstances, they may have failed to provide you with the attention you require.

Suffering is inherent in the human experience. However, we all have the opportunity to grow through — and out of — our suffering. Reparenting yourself is an effective way to accomplish this. And you can begin right now.

Reparent Your Inner Child and Heal Trauma

Some of us still seek someone "out there" to console our inner children. It's easy to think everything will be fine once you find the right partner, soul mate, or spiritual community.

However, this is typically a Band-Aid solution. Other people can only comfort your inner child if they act following your expectations. Old wounds come to the surface when they do something that isn't on your agenda. You return to your suffering.

That is why inner child work is so effective. It enables you to become your parent by consciously working with childhood trauma. You learn to give yourself the loving attention you need to heal.

And you don't have to rely on anyone for that.

Although techniques come in all shapes and sizes, working with your inner child can be broken down into three general steps: connect, communicate, and nurture.

First, you must recognize the child within. You can't start the healing process if it goes unnoticed.

Then you begin conversing with it. Finding a specific way to hear what the inner child has to say is essential for gaining access to the source of your trauma.

Finally, you assume the role of a caring parent. You give your inner child self exactly what it requires as an adult.

Inner child work is frequently done in collaboration with a therapist. However, if your trauma isn't too severe or you've already done some inner work, I'm confident you can complete much of this work on your own.

I've included some helpful hints below. Although I haven't finished my healing process, I've learned much.

These recommendations are based on my personal experience and inner child work with my therapist. I hope they can be of assistance to you.

1.   Connect

You might not know where to begin if you decide to reparent yourself. If connecting with your inner child sounds enigmatic, I have good news.

The first step can be very useful.

The main goal is to become more aware of who you were as a child. To do so, gather information about what you did, where you spent the time, what you liked, and who you were.

Speak with people who knew you back then, such as family members and childhood friends, to gather more information. You can also look through old photos of yourself. Pay close attention to the details. Take note of what you're wearing, how you're standing, who you're talking to, and so on.

The more you think about your childhood, the more you'll be able to feel how you did back then. Knowing how you look can also help you talk to your inner child, which is the next step in the process.

2. Communicate.

Although your inner child communicates with you daily, the messages may be missed. We miss even the most obvious cues when engrossed in our daily routines.

As a result, making time to communicate with your inner child is essential. This can be accomplished through self-discovery practices like meditation or journaling.

I did it with the help of a visualization exercise with my therapist. She walked me through it, but you can do it alone.

Close your eyes and sit in a quiet, comfortable room. Imagine yourself as a 5-7-year-old — or whatever age you believe your trauma occurred. Allow the child to express their distress. Allow them to cry, yell, or do whatever they want.

It may also help to visualize a specific setting or people you believe are connected to your trauma, such as your parents. The more specific you do this exercise, the easier it will be to empathize with the inner child.

You may ask the following questions once you have

vividly seen your child self:

- What is the child in front of you thinking?

- What do they require?

- What are they judging, blaming, or shaming themselves about?

- What are you willing to forgive them for right now?

- What could you say to encourage that child?

You are not required to ask all of those questions at once. Your child will notice a difference even if you only ask one question. It will appear that someone is concerned.

3. Develop

The final step is to give your inner child what he or she needs most. This is often about meeting the two emotional needs we all have in our first years: the need to feel safe and the need to feel loved no matter what.

You can do this by keeping up with the visualization exercise from the last step. Think about holding the child in your arms, stroking their hair, or doing something loving for them. By imagining this, you put yourself in the role of your parent. You instill feelings of love and safety in your inner child, which he or she desperately requires.

Reinforcing positive self-talk and beliefs is another way to nurture your child. That is something I enjoy doing in front of a mirror. This provides me with a visual cue that allows me to externalize my inner child and care for it as a loving parent.

Sit in front of the mirror and examine yourself. Don't forget that these are the same eyes you had as a child. They can help you get in touch with your inner child.

What do they need to hear?

You can say it out loud or think it in your head. No matter what, use words and a tone of voice that a caring parent would use. Remember that your inner child is paying attention. What you say could help it get over its past hurts. It will soon come out to play, innocent and joyful.

CHAPTER 11
WHAT IS SPIRITUALITY?

Spirituality is a big idea that can be understood in many different ways. In general, it means feeling like we belong to something bigger than ourselves and looking for meaning in our lives. As a result, it is something that everyone goes through and affects us all. A spiritual experience can be called sacred, transcendent, or just a strong feeling of being alive and connected to everything else.

Some people's spiritual lives may be inextricably linked to their affiliation with a church, temple, mosque, or synagogue. Others may find comfort in prayer, a personal relationship with God, or a higher power. Others look for meaning in their connections to nature or art. Your definition of spirituality, like your sense of purpose, may change throughout your life as you adapt to your own experiences and relationships.

Spiritual concerns

Many people associate spirituality with questions

about life and identity, such as "Am I a great person?"

- What is the significance of my pain?

- What is my relationship to the world around me?

- Do events occur for a reason?

- How can I live my life to its fullest potential?

Religion and spirituality and their relationship

While spirituality may include religious elements, it is generally a broader concept. Religion and spirituality are not synonymous, nor are they opposed. The best way to visualize this is to imagine two overlapping circles like this:

- The questions in spirituality are: where do I find meaning, connection, and value?

- The questions in religion are: what is true and right?

The individual experience is where the circles overlap, influencing how you think, feel, and behave.

Spirituality vs emotional well-being

As you read, you'll notice that many practices for

cultivating spirituality are also recommended for improving emotional well-being. All aspects of well-being, including emotional and spiritual ones, influence and overlap, which is why the two are so intertwined.

Peace, awe, contentment, gratitude, and acceptance are positive emotions resulting from a spiritual quest to connect to something bigger than oneself.

Maintaining a healthy emotional state requires developing a worldview that allows you to see and appreciate your place in a greater whole. Therefore, the spiritual and the emotional are not the same thing but are deeply intertwined.

CONCLUSION
BELIEFS DETERMINE YOUR LIFE

We all have beliefs, ranging from Father Christmas when we are children to God or religion when we are adults.

Beliefs and what we believe in various aspects of our lives shape our DECISIONS daily.

Other beliefs influence our choices, such as relationships, friends, food, and lifestyle. We will never be able to change them and improve the quality of our lives unless we become aware of them and how they affect our lives.

1. Self-Esteem

What do you think of yourself? Do you believe you have unlimited capacity and opportunity, or do you have limited capacity and opportunity? Perhaps you believe that "money does not grow on trees" or that "children should be seen rather than heard." Some of these are beliefs passed down from our parents, possibly from their grandparents, and may or may not be true! However, we continue to believe them because it is "all we know" and "learned behavior."

These self-beliefs, if not addressed, can have daily consequences on your life and the decisions you make - on a moment-to-moment basis.

Make time today to write down a positive statement or belief for each of the abovementioned areas.

Here are a couple of examples:

1. CONFIDENCE IN ONESELF - "I am enough, I love myself, and I value my life."

2. A POSITIVE food belief - "I enjoy eating all foods in moderation, eating as naturally as possible, and drinking alcohol in moderation."

3. A POSITIVE fitness belief - "When I put in the effort to exercise for 10 minutes a day, I always feel the benefits and am glad I did it."

"You have everything you need within you now to improve your life quality," I believe after reading this book.

What do you think?

www.ingramcontent.com/pod-product-compliance
Lightning Source LLC
LaVergne TN
LVHW051111180726
843512LV00011B/793